AF322630

Blood & Betrayal

Anna Elizabeth, Sasha Joy

A Vampire's Blood by Anna Elizabeth

The Vampire's Betrayal by Sasha Joy

Contents

A Vampire's Blood

A Vampire's Blood
Part 1

A Vampire's Blood

Part 1

My name is Jess, short for Jessica Lynn. I'm far from normal. Brown eyes and wavy brown hair with pale skin, petite, would be considered normal in appearance. In my case, I'm a nineteen-year-old girl who is far from normal. Living a life of the same routine on a daily basis was all about to change.

You see, I carry vampire blood within my veins, but I am human, at least I was, at that present time. I would like to relate my story to you of this 'struggle' I've endured since my childhood. The choices I've had to make, or should I say, the one fatal choice I had to make. This is my story...

I was raised in Central Alabama along the wooded area of a small country town. Oak trees went on for miles, with their hunter green leaves blowing in the soothing wind. Rabbits, deer, and other various creatures survive within these secluded woods.

Our home is in the center of all this greenery, the browns of the tree trunks. The house was a cozy, peaceful structure having a wraparound porch with a country-like style. White cedar posts connected to the arched roof to support this lovely dwelling, which rested upon the dirty white banisters of the ancient porch. Such a quiet, undisturbed place for one to dwell.

A perfect location for a young girl to grow up in. I used to play for here, having childish adventures, running through the mysterious woods, talking to the squirrels within my enchanted forest, and pretending in a make-believe way, as if these animals were my royal siblings. A wonderful habitation for my imagination to run wild, free.

I always loved picking the colorful wildflowers that grew along the edges of the yard near the grassy wood line. I constantly brought a handful of these flowers, weeds mostly, into the house giving them to my mother, who would put them graciously in a decorative vase with iced water and place them on the center of the kitchen table. I would smile a big smile every time I'd see my mother making a big deal out of the beauty of these so-called flowers that I would bring her. She would sneeze several times as she laughed out loud, then she'd hug me and remind me of how much she loved me.

Eventually, my mother explained the difference between actual flowers and ragweed. She helped me to understand that these types of weeds look remarkably like beautiful flowers; that I was gathering wild ragweed that caused severe allergies.

That's when Mother surprised me with roses, planting them all along the front porch. They were red as fire, deep crimson, with the most gorgeous red petals.

Mother expressed to me how much these flowers reminded her of blood since they were so dark and red. These big roses smelled amazing; with the scent they gave out. Running wild along the porch banisters, these roses dressed the appearance of the house up making it seem more elegant.

Living here with just my mother; I never knew my father, only the vague tales my mother would tell me about him. She would always say he was a handsome man, well-dressed, and an exceptional distinguished gentleman. She assured me that he would've loved me if he had got to meet me.

You see, Mother explained to me that when I was quite young my father was killed just shortly after I was born. She constantly painted a brief picture of him, an image for my imagination, of who he was and how he looked, but never spoke cruelly of him. Sometimes Mother would shed a tear down her cheek when she spoke about him. Her stories never were lengthy when speaking of my father. It saddened her every time I'd ask about him, but she would respond with a saddened smile. My mother, I believed, truly loved my father.

The one question I would ask on many occasions was how my father was killed, but she would change the subject and avoid answering me. I was around twelve years of age before she finally told me how my father was killed.

During my childhood, my mother unremittingly encouraged me to be who I was no matter the ridicule. The children from my school would make fun of me, calling me horrible names, pushing and shoving me down all the time while laughing at me as they pointed their fingers at me. Saying cruel gestures about my mother and making her out to be false things such as 'witch' or 'possessed by the devil'. Rumors were shouted at me about how my father was killed but his body was never discovered. Some of the kids would say that my father was sacrificed by my mother to the devil himself, while others would shout that my father was brutally murdered by my mother for his riches. These speculations would eventually make me cry.

Mother being the mild-mannered lady that she was, would reassure me comforting me daily by telling me it wasn't much truth to any of the lies these adolescents would speak of. She would always say that we were different, free spirited, special, and perfect. Those cruel people with their children were just jealous and confused since we were happy living the way we lived. They just did not understand us. The didn't understand our ways due to their closed, narrow minds. They couldn't comprehend how our wonderful lives together was so peaceful living out here in our private, little piece of paradise within our own small kingdom. I felt better every time after hearing my mother's soothing words, besides, my mother would always end this conversation with ice cream before dinner and a loving hug.

When I started my junior high days, the cruelty of my fellow students became much harsher. They began to lash out at me a lot more than before, and it all related to my mother. Calling me vulgar names and 'the witch's daughter', 'spawn of Satan', and 'that weird demon of a girl'. That's when my mother took me out of school and began homeschooling me. She figured it was best since I started fighting the kids back at school, defending myself and my mother's name.

I did finish my high school studies and graduated with an advanced diploma. I enjoyed my daily lessons and learning at home without all the ridicule from other students. It was nice to have my mother as my teacher. She was exceptional person when it came to teaching me. She taught me more about nature, how to grow herbs, and the meanings of each herbal plant. She was confident that I needed to know about the quality of herbal healing, our earth, and how to care for it. I must admit, I thoroughly enjoyed these lessons on nature, all the different herbs, and the plants that grow from the soil within the earth's ground. I thought it interesting how such herbs could be so healthy to one's body.

After I received my diploma in the mail, my mother celebrated by decorating the house with fake flowers of various colors and ribbons. She performed a small ceremony in my honor. I had to walk through the house and receive my diploma while wearing a nice sun dress and a crown of daisies on my head. My mother snapped pictures of me with her camera as she cried tears of pure joy. It was awkward, but I felt accomplished and that I could be anything I desired in this life. I was proud to have her as my mentor and my mother.

As I grew into a mature teenager, a young adult, I buried my inner emotions into painting and various arts. I fell in love with this trade at once. Mother was convinced that I had a special 'talent' for painting. She bought me a canvas and some paints, and it all started from there. I often spent my time in front of my canvas expressing myself through the colors of the paint as they would splash across the bare context. Roses were my favorite thing to design on my canvas, along with the scenery of the woods and sky. I rarely ever picked up a paint brush, I would use my fingertips to draft the roses and the layout of the wood line.

Mother would thrill me by making me feel like a true artist. She would hang my works of art throughout the house, pretty much on every wall. She told me that they bring her much pleasure to see them and that it made her heart happier to know I was doing something I loved.

As I said earlier, I was around twelve years of age when my mother finally talked to me about my father's death. It came about when my mother noticed I was having issues with hungering for blood. Not quite understanding this strange urge, I thought I was going insane, losing my mind, or that something was severely wrong with me. Not really telling my mother about any of these cravings, I would only run to my bedroom slamming the door when this unknown urge arose inside my chest. I thought within my child-like brain that I was dying, or possibly going crazy, like a mental patient.

Mother recognized my symptoms right away. That's when she gently explained the entire reasoning for these sudden impulses as she sat beside me on my canopy bed holding my hand gracefully in hers. She gestured for me to follow her to the front porch...

My mother was a beautiful, exquisite lady with hair so bright and blonde, and her eyes were blue as the morning sky. Her complexion was pale, like porcelain white. Her voice was calming and soothing in nature even when she was upset or angered. She always had a soft touch when it came to my discipline. I can honestly say that I've never been 'spanked' by my mother or anyone, for that matter. She would rather talk to me instead in a mild mannered, loving way helping me to understand what it was that I had done wrong. This method worked best for me because I always felt guilty inside after hearing my mother's words.

Her appearance and her apparel were fascinating to me as a child, with her long boho-style skirts and her beaded necklaces made of turquoise hanging around her neck. She unceasingly wore a turquoise ring on her index finger with a dull silver finished band. She incessantly promised this gorgeous ring to me on the day I turn sixteen. She even had a ceremony on my birthday when she presented it to me. It was a cherished memory for me, so imaginative...

Decorative lights and pillar candles were strolled through the entire house. Mother held my hand walking me through in a circle of the house, seating me on the little ottoman in the living room. She gave me a tiny speech, "I give this trinket of a ring in love and great gratitude to my one and only daughter, the blood of my blood. May the God of the Heavens bless this token of peace and happiness to my beautiful, free-spirited child. I love you honey; always cherish this ring and keep it close to your heart. May it remind you of my undying love for you."

Smiling as big as I could, I gladly accepted this turquoise ring placing it on my thumb. I will, forever, keep this little trinket. Although, it's faded quite a bit over the years, I still continue to wear my mother's ring.

So, you see, my mother was a ceremonial person who completed her tasks in life with compassion and love. She was the reason I had such a vivid imagination.

Now back to the night that my mother explained her secret of my father's death...

Mother revealed to me on that cloudy, overcast night, as we were resting comfortably on our front porch swing while she continued to hold my hand in hers. With a slight cool breeze passing by, she spoke the words, "I am immortal, honey. An undead creature of the night, a vampire."

Laughing out loud, I thought she was teasing me, but I realized she was being very serious by the look on her unsettling, stern face. After pondering on her words to me for a few seconds, I decided these words to be true. I remembered back on how Mother would only surface from her bedroom, that contained heavily draped curtains, just past sundown. Her room was always dark, and she never really seemed to eat any food, even when we would be seated at the dining room table while she watched me eat my meals. It all seemed to make better sense now.

Of course, Mother did not sleep in a coffin. She had a lovely queen-sized bed in her well-darkened room, along with nice, silk bedding attire.

I recalled having a 'nanny', but only vaguely. It wasn't until I was able to care for myself on a regular, daily routine that this 'nanny' went away. That would explain why I had to tend to myself at the age of seven, awaiting my mother to wake up every evening around dusk. As a young child, I didn't know any other way to live, only what I was taught. In my adolescent mind, I figured all the other kids lived in the same manner. Even on school mornings, I caught the school bus while Mother was still sleeping, but there was always a sack-lunch prepared and waiting for me on the dining room table. After school each day, I would do my homework and play outside in the woods or something until the sun fell behind the horizon. When I came inside my mother would be awake preparing some type of meal for me. When I went to bed each night, I would hear her leave the house. Now I understand why she left and didn't return until several hours later.

Anyway, Mother had decided it was time I knew the truth about who I was and about what happened to my father and to her. She figured since I was only twelve, it might be hard to comprehend, but she knew I was mature for my age, so she wanted to tell me everything about the past...

"What I'm about to tell you, Jessica Lynn, will make everything clearer." Mother began her story. "I was a young, giddy girl of only thirteen, living in the back bayous of New Orleans with my aunt and my cousins. My parents had given me over to my aunt which gladly accepted taking me in. My parents wanted to travel the world but didn't need a child hindering their journey. They did not want the hassle of trying to raise a kid and take care of one while on their travels. They swore they loved me, but I never heard from them after they left me with my aunt. I never laid eyes on them again.

One late evening, my cousins, who became my siblings, and I were playing childish games while dancing around the small firepit we created in the yard. We were dancing and singing make-believe songs as the boisterous bonfire blazed. That's when I was distracted by a strange noise I heard from just inside the woods. Curious to see what the noise could have been, maybe a small animal, or something interesting or hurt. Along the way between the vicious swamp and the shaded wood line, I followed this mysterious sound.

As the evening grew darker with only the pale moonlight to see, and the voices of my cousins singing in the background faded, I realized I had wandered too far away. In fear, I found I was lost in this mindless darkness with only the moon to guide me. Shaking inside, I knew I was dreadfully in danger. I hadn't any idea which way to turn or which way to find my path home. The mystery sound I was searching for ceased and all I could hear were the swamp animals in the darkness. Stumbling over a large tree root along my path next to the flowing waters of the swamp, I tumbled forward hitting my head on the dirty soil below. Passing out from such a blow to my forehead, I was oblivious to the faint creature that vaguely appeared as it stood over me. My eyes went dark as they shut, and I was unconscious.

Awakening the next morning when the bright sunlight touched my face, I was disillusioned at my surroundings." Mother continued. "After moments of silence within this swamp, I finally regained my composure as I realized I was still lost. I had laid in these woods all night! Jumping to my feet, I scanned the area as I became aware of exactly where I was. It was simply too hard to distinguish where I had walked to in the dark, but now the sun was out and I could see better,

I knew my way back to the house. My head throbbed from falling and hitting it, but I had to get home.

Quickly, I ran straight to my house and went hurriedly to my bedroom crawling under the blankets on my bed. I noticed that no one was stirring yet, and they didn't even notice I was missing the entire night. Everyone was fast asleep. No one had searched for me. Even the next few days, no one asked where I had been or even acted like I was gone that night, like I hadn't been missing at all.

Touching my neck with my fingertips, I felt blood on the surface of my skin. At that instant, my throat started aching severely as I noticed blood on my fingertips. Something had bitten me. At that time, I didn't understand what it could had been that bit me, but over the next few months, I started to have blood hungers and urges to taste blood. I thought I was becoming insane. Of course, I never fed on anyone or any animal, but the strange hunger was there. It would come and go at different moments.

One such instance, I was looking in the refrigerator for something to drink when I saw a pack of chicken breast thawing on the shelf. My aunt was planning to make a big dinner for all of us that evening. I stared at the blood underneath the raw chicken for several minutes. I was tempted to taste it, but my aunt came into the kitchen and yelled at me to close the frig door. Slamming the door of the frig, I hastily bolted outside behind a tree on the edge of the yard. Crying and nervous, I knew I couldn't tell my aunt or my cousins about any of this. They would think I was nuts, or just making up silly tales. So, I kept it to myself, hidden deep within my own thoughts. Some days were harder than most days, to resist the sudden strong urges for blood.

It was after I was much older that I moved and relocated in Alabama. After steady research, I discovered that it was a vampire who had bit me that scary night. I still remember his ugly face before I passed out that frightening night. I assumed I was hallucinating, but it really was something looking at me. It had to be real, vampires existed. It was the only explanation for such blood hungers that I was having. All through my days of becoming an adult back on that bayou, I fought such pangs of hunger until I left at the age of seventeen. That's when I met your father.

I had gone to a picture show in the small town. I fell madly in love with him at first sight. He was standing in front of me in the ticket line before I went in to watch the show. He looked at me and it began from there. After several romantic dates and intense flirting, I gave in and married him.

The strong blood hungers ceased after marrying him. We settled here in this place shortly after we were married. Your father purchased this land from his uncle and built this very house we are living in now. Finding out thereafter that I was pregnant with you, Jessica Lynn, my dearest love. We were happy and content in our little abode.

The night of your birth was when everything changed. Having a home birth, your father helped deliver you, Jess. You were the most stunning baby girl we had ever imagined having. You favored your father more, with that deep brown hair and those pretty, brown eyes. You were our little miracle, our amazing blessing from above."

Mother explained further, "It was days later, I was holding you in my arms as I rocked you gently in the mahogany rocking chair, that the severe blood hunger returned. I had forgotten about it. Your father came home after a long day of work, only to find I was a complete mess. I was so tormented by this hunger, it seemed unbearable, a lot worse than before. You were fast asleep in your baby crib when I brutally attacked your father draining him of all the blood in his body. Disposing of his corpse, I buried him deep in the woods. Local authorities concluded he was a missing person, but the case stayed unsolved. That's why the people in town ridicule you so much, Jess. They suspect his disappearance to be murderous, but they would never understand the truth of his disappearance. I've been a vampire ever since, feeding on mortal blood, on occasion, as the need arises.

The same 'struggle' is now yours to bear, Jessica Lynn. This vampire blood flows within your veins. I was hoping it would not be so, but I see the signs of such hunger developing in you. This whole thing is like a curse, but I hate that word, so, I call it our 'struggle'. You can control it but it's not easy some days. The best advice I can give you is, never fall in love and bear a child, or the same fate could befall you." Mother concluded.

So, this is where my story actually begins. You could imagine as a child of only twelve years of age how bizarre that information could've been. I've lived with this 'struggle', this knowledge ever since. I wanted to believe it was all a horrid fairytale that my mother had told me, but this 'struggle' was real. My mother was a vampire, and I carried that same blood in my veins. Although I never experienced the sight of my mother as she would feed on a human, I knew it to be so. I secluded myself away from socializing with other kids my age for this exact reason. Understand more why the children from my former school would say such nasty things to me. Yet, they didn't know the true story of my mother, and what happened to my father. I knew what they would say was all lies, just vicious rumors, so I did not let it hurt me anymore. Mother was right, we were different but extremely special. I was proud of who my mother was, her nature was good-hearted and honest. She was merely surviving. It was not her fault what happened to her, turning into this horrid creature, who can only survive on blood alone.

Mostly, I stayed home hanging out with Mother, avoiding the self-ish kids in town, yet I did enjoy Mother's company, especially, her friendship.

Now, you see, therefore, why I poured myself into my art. I felt free, relieved, like a different person every time I painted. My mother always encouraged me to paint what I felt, and what I loved. She understood me.

I had fun times with Mother though when she wasn't working all night on her computer. That was her way of making a living from home, electronic sales online. She was my best friend and confidant. She always supported me emotionally and she loved me greatly.

One such memory of my mother's full support towards me was when I was in grade school. There was a girl in my class who was popular with the other kids including the teacher. She was always getting along with the other students and showing them favorable attention. This girl never paid much attention to me though. She would always roll her eyes at me in passing and persuade the other kids to stay clear of me. I wasn't quite aware at the time as to why this girl was so harsh toward me, but I would soon come to understand why.

One morning in class, this same girl was handing out invitations to her masquerade birthday party at her home on the weekend. As she strolled past each desk handing the other students an invitation, she slipped right past my desk as she rolled her eyes at me going to the next desk behind me. I felt so awful! I only put my head down in my arms upon my desk so that no one could see my tears. Later that evening at home, Mother could see something was bothering me.

She asked me several times if I was okay, but I only told her that I was fine. Finally, Mother kept up her nagging and I revealed what was upsetting me. I told her about the girl from school and how she passed by my desk rolling her eyes. Mother only chuckled a small laugh.

"Jess, don't let that little girl ruin your happiness!" Mother stated. "If it's a masquerade party you want to attend, then we will have one here. This Saturday, we will celebrate a birthday unlike any other birthday!"

I smiled a small grin as I wiped my warm tears from my face. Mother always knew how to encourage me. It wasn't even close to being my birthday, but I was thrilled to pretend that it was!

Mother gave me the biggest hug as she said, "Now, let's go to town and get all the decorations, Jess."

That following Saturday, Mother held true to her word. She decorated the house and even made us costumes. Mother wore a nice satin, white gown with lace trimmed on the edges. She wore a pearl, white mask with small pearls along the top of it. She fixed her hair up high on her head with pastel pink feathers strolled throughout. My costume consisted of a pink satin dress with florals designed in the material. Mother made me a mask of pastel pink with slight fuzzy feathers edged on the rim of it. These feathers tickled my nose, but I did not care. I loved my costume and my mask!

Mother celebrated by making cupcakes of various flavors and designs! We enjoyed the sweets and some fancy ginger ale in crystal champagne glasses. Mother played ballroom music throughout the house as we danced long into the night hours. It was such a magical experience for me. Mother tucked me in my bed that night as I still wore my mask, saying, " I love you, Jess, my little angel."

I still have the mask Mother made for me. I will forever cherish it!

Everything was going smoothly. It all changed after I started my first job in town. After intense begging, my mother finally agreed to let me go to work, part-time.

Excited and nervous, the first day at my job was at the art gallery in the middle of the main street. I was the receptionist at the front counter. As agreed, the owner said I could display one of my paintings here, changing it out once a month. That was so exciting to me! Bringing my best painting to hang in the gallery, I decided to use the one with all the red roses across the lattice porch with a beautiful blue sky painted above the old country house, with whites, greens, and blues within the painting. It was my favorite piece of art I painted.

Getting to hang my picture just above the side wall entrance, I was thrilled! I get the pleasure of looking at it every day I'm at work, just knowing it's my creation for others to see excited me.

Upon settling in at my station, I promptly got the hang of answering phones and greeting the people as they came in to view the gallery of exquisite art and such. I must admit I loved this line of work. My shift consisted of four days a week, split shifts between mornings and afternoons. It was a stress-free environment, with the people being friendly, and getting to socialize, a little, with someone other than my mother. It seemed to be the change I needed. That was until...

One afternoon at my post, I was daydreaming about my paintings being well known. Pretending in my mind that I was the next Picasso. That's when my thoughts were interrupted. He walked in. This guy with sandy, blonde hair, and the cutest eyes I had ever seen. He was tall and lean, with just the right amount of muscle tone. I believe my mouth even dropped open a little.

As this gorgeous man approached my counter, I found I was tongue-tied. Choking on my words, I finally was able to utter, "Hello, sir. I'm Jess. How can I help you?"

He greeted me properly, giving me his name, which was Chris. His smile was fascinating! He wanted to buy a ticket to view the gallery. Getting my composure back in check, I happily volunteered to show him around. Learning, in small talk, that his uncle owned this art gallery, and he was here to visit for a while. Passing under the display of my painting, he spoke, "Now, that piece of art is exquisite. I like the floral look of the darkened roses across the porch of the old country house."

"Really?" I asked as I smiled selfishly. "Thank you! I did that piece."

It all started from there. I got quite acquainted with Chris from this point on. Almost daily, we would hang out, after my shift, at the little coffee shop across the street, talking on and on about art and literature. We had so much in common, subjects of art, and artists. I discovered a great deal of information about him. For one thing, he was a lover of art just as I was. Although he couldn't paint well, he still enjoyed the meanings behind each piece of art that was created. I commenced telling him about my creation in the art gallery. He appeared extremely fascinated by my words on it. He seemed so intrigued by what inspired me to paint that masterpiece, as he called it. I went on telling him about my home and the little kingdom of Heaven where I was raised. Of my mother and how we were very close in friendship. Of course, I left out the whole vampire part and the hunger for blood part. I realized I was going on about myself, so I asked him about himself.

He was a student at the National Museum of Fine Arts, upstate. He would be in town only a short, few months, visiting his uncle. He was raised in north Alabama, so he wasn't too familiar with the area. He knew where the park and the little apartment complex were because he resided near it and where his uncle's art gallery was located on the main street, the only street in town that wasn't a dirt road.

I thoroughly enjoyed our talks, our conversations, and our time together. Knowing in my mind, we could be such good friends. Emotionally, I had to stay aware that vampire blood remained inside of me. I could not allow any such feelings to go beyond friendship. Feeling I could control myself; I figured having a real friend wasn't that harmful. Other than the friendship with my mother, Chris was my first and only friend.

Deciding not to mention this newfound friend to my mother, for I knew she would argue against it. Besides, I had it covered, all under self-control.

At home that night, Mother kept eyeballing me as if I was keeping something from her, but I played it off avoiding any type of deep conversation. Telling her I was exhausted from work today so I will just go to bed early tonight. She would only nod her head, smiling, knowing I was telling her a little white lie.

Trying to sleep as I lay in my bed, I kept having thoughts about Chris and I's conversation from earlier. It was amazing for me to get to talk with someone other than my mother. I felt like I have grown as an adult now. Like I could have a normal life, a happy life with real friends and real conversations.

Awaiting Chris, one late afternoon, right before the sun went down, at the coffee shop, for our routine visit, I found myself in a daze, a lustful thinking daze. Pondering on his sensational blue eyes, his masculine, physical well-being. Catching myself, I knew better than to think these thoughts, but I couldn't help it. I was getting attached to our little talks, our special connection that I felt every time we would meet for coffee. I enjoyed his presence, and I had to get a grip on my emotions or this whole friendship would have to come to a halt.

As we sat here discussing politics, art, and various other subjects, I understood within myself that I was falling for this guy. Though I did not want to admit it, it was happening, and I was 'struck' by him.

Feeling warm and funny in the pit of my stomach, like I had butterflies swarming around, I panicked. I hastily excused myself, rushing home, leaving Chris in mid-sentence, speechless.

Mother knew as soon as I came in that something was bothering me.

"Jess, are you okay?' Mother asked curiously. "You seem upset, paranoid."

"Mother, I have a confession to make." I choked timidly, feeling like I was hyperventilating. "I met someone in town at the art gallery a few weeks back, that I haven't mentioned to you yet. A friendship started, and I thought it was all going well until today. I caught myself feeling more intense, physical attraction toward him. It frightened me, so I left him sitting there and came straight home. I feel so bad for rushing out on him, the way I did, but I had no choice."

"I see." Mother responded as she rubbed her chin with her hand. "Okay. Jessica Lynn, let me make us a cup of herbal tea, and we can talk."

Sipping the warm tea eased my nerves quite a bit. Mother only held her hands around her cup of tea, smelling the steamy aroma of it, as she explained what I knew she would say; how I should end this friend zone and never meet with this guy again.

It wasn't so simple as that. I knew in my heart that I would see him again. I wanted, desperately, to see him, at least once more, to truthfully confess my feelings to him, and to touch his face with my hand. I wanted to feel his lips upon my lips. But there was no way I could express all these feelings in my head to my mother. So, instead, I only agreed that she was probably right. Hugging me tightly, Mother said, "I will help get you through this, Jess. I'm here for you, as I will be forever."

"I know, Mother," I replied. "I appreciate your help, but I think I will be fine. I always am."

Lying in my bed that night, my thoughts were still dwelling on Chris. Hoping he's not upset with me for bailing out on him today.

How could I ever explain to him why I left so fast? I wonder if I'm just being foolish. Would Chris even feel the same feelings for me?

My mind shifted, thinking about my mother when she fell in love with my father. Trying to imagine, visualize, how it could've been. It must have been amazing to know that kind of love, but how could I possibly love Chris, taking his life later in the relationship? The mere thought of having a child with him frightened me, let alone killing him afterward.

Making myself push these bizarre thoughts out of my mind, I closed my eyes and drifted into a deep, dreamless sleep.

Waking up near midnight, I made my way, sluggishly, into the kitchen to get a drink of tap water. Finding my mother sitting at the little dinette table, I noticed her face had blood on it. Impulsively, I ran over to her, asking, "Mother, are you okay?"

"I'm all right, Jess." Mother responded calmly, smiling as her fangs showed marginally under her lip. "You caught me unaware. I just got home from feeding, sweetie. Don't be alarmed, it's not my blood, it's just some miserable homeless, drugged-out man from the city. This is his blood. Let me go clean my face and then we can talk."

Speechless, I just stood there. That was the first time I'd seen her like this. Mother could see the shocked, stunned expression of concern on my face in this dim kitchen, with only the moonlight peeking through the window above the sink.

I wasn't sure what to think, or how to imagine what she did to that wretched homeless man. Knowing she's a vampire, it still bothered me, unsettled me, for some strange reason. The mere thought of someone being killed by my mother was vaguely disturbing.

Mother returned, turning on the tabletop lamp near the dinette table, and we both seated ourselves at the table. Before I could speak, Mother spoke instead, "Jess, it's okay. It's who I am, you already know this. I've had to keep it hidden from you for as long as I could. This is exactly what you will become if you continue to see that boy. The blood urge will, possibly, get stronger for you every time you are around that young man. Just think about it before you put yourself in that kind of circumstance, sweetie. I just don't want to see you make the same mistake I made, and must live for eternity regretting it, feeling guilty for it."

Kissing my mother's forehead, I walked back to my room, without giving her a response, pondering what she just said. I had to make myself fall back asleep. I refused to think any more about all this until tomorrow.

Morning finally came, and I was in my same, usual, routine as I made my way to the art gallery to do my duty as the receptionist. Still weighing my situation with Chris back and forth in my mind. The day was slow, with barely anyone visiting the gallery. Nodding off and on with this sleepy composure, I awakened when the little gold bell chimed from the front entrance of the gallery. You guessed it, Chris was walking straight to my station.

"Jess, can we talk?" Chris asked so politely, with a hint of irritation in his voice. "I've already spoken to my uncle, and he allowed you to take the rest of the day off since it's so slow in here."

"I suppose that'd be good," I responded lightly as I gathered my purse, yawning.

I knew where this conversation was headed, but there was no avoiding it. Might as well get it over with.

We went to our usual spot at the coffee shop across the street from the gallery, ordered two vanilla lattes, and seated ourselves at the little coffee table outside.

"I will start first. Jess, what happened yesterday?" Chris pleaded. "I tried calling you several times, but you wouldn't answer."

"It was just a family thing, but it's okay now." I replied apologetically, trying to sound calm, yet I only wanted to scream out 'I can't be with you, because I might kill you later.' I'm so sorry for running away like that. I'm okay now, really, I am."

"Good, but don't you ever do that to me again." He said, smiling as he reached over, placing my hand in his.

"I promise, I won't." I retorted as I smiled back at him, looking at his face, his adorable face.

We chatted for what seemed like hours about petty nonsense, and the latest art expenditures of various artists, when I decided to assess the waters; I just couldn't stand it anymore. I needed to see if I was the only one feeling this way, or if he felt the same in return. The whole time I sat here, I couldn't help but heed my mother's words, but I so wanted to know how he felt. Having 'butterflies' come back in my stomach, I was affected to find out, stubbornly determined.

"Chris, I have to know something," I stated unwavering. "I've been feeling this connection between us lately. I think I'm starting to fall for you a little. Am I being silly for thinking this?"

Not saying a word back to me, Chris stood and leaned over the table, kissing me. Shocked, I found myself kissing him back. That was my first real kiss! It was so amazing!

After our little kiss, he asked as he looked straight into my eyes, "Would you like to take a walk to the park? Yes, Jess, I do feel the same about you. I knew I liked you the first moment I laid eyes on you in the art gallery."

Smiling, I at once nodded my head as if to say yes.

Strolling hand in hand through the park, like high school kids, I was feeling joyful; we talked more about how we both felt about each other. Learning that he thought my brown eyes were the prettiest eyes he had ever seen. He even liked the way I would snort a little when I laughed too hard.

Laughing, smiling, and flirting like a couple who just found 'puppy' love; we kissed often, holding hands the entire time.

The day turned out to be my most wonderful day ever! It started slow and dreary but turned out to be an amazing one! The park was full of people, yet it felt like we were the only ones there.

Inviting me back to his humble apartment to make dinner, I quickly said yes. I didn't want to let this blessed day end. I was so happy, yet I was somewhat scared at the same time.

Afraid of being with him, of loving him, but I knew I would be okay. I must control the blood hunger urges if they arise. Afraid, that while near him like I am now, this wretched hunger could sprout out of nowhere. I refuse to allow such a thing to happen, even if it hurts me instead! I will be with this man. That's just the way it will have to be. I reject passing up this one-time chance at falling in love and being happy, even if it's only for a short time. Just a risky chance I must take now.

Helping Chris prepare dinner was enjoyable. We made grilled cheese sandwiches with French fries with wine to drink. Of course, I did not have but one glass of this red wine. Sitting down to dinner we talked and laughed about all kinds of subjects that had unimportant meanings.

After dinner we sat on his little blue love seat as we put a typical comedy on. Snuggled together throughout the movie Chris was a perfect gentleman. I realized it was getting late and Mother had no idea where I was. I was caught up in this amazing day and I forgot to let her know I would be a while getting home.

As I was leaving through his entrance door, he pulled me by my hand closer to him. Placing his hands onto my cheeks he gently kissed my lips. It was the best kiss in the world to me. Feelings of lust and desire flowed through my entire body. Hesitating, as long as I could, I thought it best to make my leave now. Besides, what kind of girl would I be giving in to this desire inside me on the first date. So, I dreadfully headed home to tell Mother about Chris.

Arriving home, Mother was at the table in the kitchenette reading a magazine on home design. I nervously sat in the little chair across from her and said, "Sorry Mother, I'm so late. I got caught up on my date with Chris."

"I figured as much, Jess." Mother replied as she smiled but with concern. "I knew you would see that boy again. The only warning that I must give is to be careful and do not get pregnant too soon. You already know what could happen and I don't think you can handle it at this present moment. I love you, sweetie, and I'm here for you if your blood hungers arise. Just promise me you'll be careful around that guy."

"I promise, Mother." I answered. "I really do like this guy. I feel amazing every time I'm around him. We laugh, we talk, we enjoy each other's company. He was my first friend and now he's my first love, I think."

"I'm happy for you, sweetie." Mother confessed. "But just be aware whenever you are close to him. That's all I ask. Well, I'm going into the woods, and I'm going to make my way to the community a few miles from here to feed. Get you some rest and we can talk again tomorrow evening."

As Mother made her way out the front door, I went to my bedroom and got ready for my nightcap.

Lying in bed, my thoughts were on Chris. I was pondering in my mind how wonderful this day went. I couldn't wait to see him again tomorrow. I drifted into a peaceful sleep with hopes of having sweet dreams of my newfound love.

So, you see, my life has changed for the good, now. I was happy. I won't bore you with the romantic details of my intimacy, and relationship with Chris; some things are just private. Just know it was very stable, romantic, and on occasion, extremely steamy. We were a happy couple. Very much in love.

Chris finally met my mother, for the first time, one late evening for a nice dinner. It went better than I expected, at least Mother didn't murder him. She was more concerned about me, I think, but she kept it civil. I knew she only wanted what was best for me, to always protect me. She always had my back in whatever decision I made, forever being there when I stumbled and fell, but I could tell she was worried.

"So, Chris, what are your intentions with my daughter," my mother questioned as she eyeballed him. "I'd advise you to answer correctly, sir."

Nervously, Chris responded to her question, "Ma'am, I would like nothing but to date and hopefully someday build a relationship or even a marriage with your daughter. I fell for her the first moment I saw her."

"I see." Mother replied. "Make sure you keep it in that order. Now, you guys eat before the food gets too cold."

Placing ourselves around the little table, we eat while chatting about various things, laughing at Mother as she told us tales of the surrounding woods. I knew they weren't true stories, but it was humorous. She kept us entertained, although she never touched her plate of food. I'm so glad Chris didn't notice.

One of Mother's stories about the woods consisted of...

"It was shortly after father and I moved here, Jess." Mother begins her short tale. "I wasn't too familiar with the area yet. I decided to take a stroll through the woods while your father was working that day. The sun was shining bright in the sky as birds chirped all around the yard. Leaving the porch, I ventured into the woods. Singing and dancing like a girl in a fairy tale I was on an adventure. I wanted to explore every inch of these woods, our property. Making note of everything I passed, and everything I saw. Counting the bigger trees in sequence so I would always remember my path. Picking the wildflowers and returning them to the trees as I placed handfuls of them at the base of these beautiful tall towers of nature. After many trees were passed, I decided to take a rest under the old Magnolia tree with leaves so crisp and pretty white flowers so large and vibrant throughout. Relaxing and looking all around I noticed the squirrels were running about the tree limbs surrounding me, barking at each other. It was so peaceful, this feeling of connecting with nature, that I fell asleep. Awaking only to find it was sundown, rushing in haste to get back to the house, I hadn't realized how far I wandered into the woods. Doing my recount of the trees on my way out along the path, I vaguely could see in front of me. At that moment I heard a growl behind me like a bobcat making its presence known. I ran so fast, bumping into the trees and stumbling over my feet on the tree roots and the brush of the weeded grassy path. By the time I made my way out of the woods, I had bumps, scrapes, and scratches galore all over me! Jess, Your father had just arrived home, and when he saw how rough my arms and legs were scraped and scratched, he freaked out wanting to take me to the hospital. I went to laughing at myself telling him I was fine and what I had heard in the woods. Now he's laughing at me too. Fortunately for me, your father was called back to work for an emergency malfunction on the job within the hour so I had time to mend my wounds before he would panic at the mere sight of them. It was such a hilarious moment. I scared myself, I think, when I heard that animal scream out. I looked affright for a few days until the scratches began to heal. Such happy moments to remember!"

Chris and I laughed out loud as Mother smiled a mischievous grin. Thinking within my head, I'm sure it was much faster than a few days for my mother to heal. As a woman with vampire blood in her veins at the time, my mother would've healed within minutes. Even I heal fast when I get a scrape. I'm positive Mother wore bandages and band-aids for a few days to act like she was wounded.

As I concluded my thoughts, Mother spoke, "Jess, sweetie, I know you think my stories of the woods are false tales, but I promise I did not make these up."

Excusing herself, Mother mentioned she had to pick up something important in town. Of course, I knew her destination was to feed on some poor human's blood, but Chris was oblivious to it.

As I said, Chris and I were exceptionally happy. We moved in together months after admitting our feelings to each other. We settled into his small apartment in the city. He dropped out of the Fine Arts school and started collaborating with his uncle at the art gallery, pretty much taking it over and running everything for his uncle. I continued to work there also, but with a pay raise.

Mother still abided at her place in the woods. I visited her at least once every week, with her warning me on a repeated routine about controlling my blood hunger if it surfaces. Of course, Chris is still oblivious to my little blood secret, and my mother's true nature. Everything seemed in perfect harmony, like living a normal life, a normal existence. Even the hunger for blood was halted at present, but that was about to change.

Part 2

A Vampire's Blood

Part 2

One early morning, we were enjoying a delightful breakfast together when the first blood hunger, in a long while hit me. Chris and I were sitting across from each other at our kitchenette table. He had finished his breakfast of eggs and bacon with a buttered bagel and was preparing to leave for the day's duties at the art gallery. My shift wasn't until that evening, so I was planning to clean around the apartment until then. Upon his departure, he leaned into place a butterfly kiss on my forehead as I held my fairy-painted coffee cup in my hand. As soon as his lips touched my skin, the hunger shot straight through my chest. Dropping my cup to the tile floor, I gasped in fear. Of course, Chris noticed this and jumped back in shock.

"Jess, baby, are you okay?" He shouted.

"I'm okay, I think," I answered with a panicked breath. "You should go on to work, I will be simply fine. It's just the lady cramps, I believe."

"Well, if it gets too bad, you call me and I will come straight home, baby." He suggested. "Love you, baby. I will be home soon."

Nodding my head and smiling at him as he kisses my forehead once more, as he made his departure. The hunger was arising, I had to shake this off. I hurriedly rushed to the bathroom and placed myself in a cold shower, trying to control my breathing as my body felt hot like a fire in a furnace. After minutes, the urge finally subsided. I needed to contact my mother. She could help me understand how to control this. That was the first time this hunger urge was that strong.

The craving to taste blood was so robust; it had never been this intense, this hard to restrain before. It made me feel like I went out of my mind for a second, like a blank feeling with no memory attached to it.

After getting dressed, I promptly made my way across town to talk with my mother. Arriving, I found Mother asleep in her awfully darkened bedroom. Easing as quietly as possible, I retrieved the bell she kept on her nightstand and rang it. She at once opened her eyes.

"What's wrong, Jessica Lynn?" Mother asked sternly, not moving only lying there with her hands draped over her chest, her eyes staring straight to the ceiling never blinking.

"The blood hunger is back, Mother. It was so resilient, more powerful this time." I confessed in a fearful tone. "I was so afraid I was going to attack Chris when he kissed my forehead this morning."

"Maybe you should come to stay with me for a while until you learn to subdue this 'struggle' Jess." Mother offered as she rose looking at me.

Placing myself next to her on the queen size bed, I responded, "You know I won't do that. I can't be without my husband. He's my world, my everything. Mother, I truly love him. I know you warned me not to fall in love, but I have. And I'm happy. I truly am. I don't want to harm Chris in any way. There's got to be something to sustain this blood hunger, to control it. I need advice on how to manage this, to face it, Mother. How did you keep it at bay all those years with father before you were expecting me?"

Shaking her head in disbelief way, Mother told me, "It was not easy, sweetie. Somedays I stayed in the woods, occupying my mind with the animals, walking for hours, and even singing to myself. Your father thought I was weird and strange, but he never questioned me. I kept myself far away from him until it eased. Then when the hunger passed, I returned to the house. Each day, it seemed that it was growing stronger. You already know the story, Jess. I lost all control shortly after you were born. This 'struggle' will win eventually, so you must be careful around others, especially Chris. You could kill him, sweetie."

"Did father ever know about the vampire blood in your veins? Did you even want to tell him?" I asked curiously.

"No, sweetie. I never told him." Mother replied sharply. If you are thinking it would help you to tell Chris about all this, you're mistaken. It would only complicate your marriage, your life as you know it now. Chris could become frightened of you or leave you. Besides, he wouldn't understand it. To tell him would be an unwise decision, I believe, sweetie."

Mother hugged me tightly as she said, "Now go home, find something to occupy your mind constantly. Another clever idea, you should consider quitting your job at the gallery. It's probably best for you to occupy yourself at home, so you won't be around so many people during all this."

"I understand, Mother. It just isn't easy for me to quit the job that I love so much, but I know you're right. Now to think of a hobby that takes my full attention." I agreed.

"You should paint again, Jess." Mother recommended it. "I know you haven't in some time. Now would be a perfect time to start again."

"Thanks, Mother. I said as I hugged her once more. Now go back to your slumber and I will call you later tonight."

Smiling at me, Mother closed her eyes and resumed her rest.

Back at home, I pulled all my art supplies from the closet. After setting everything up, I began to paint on my canvas. My mother was right, this did help subside the urges. Spending all day painting, I completely forgot to call in sick at work. Chris came in, asking, "You all right, baby? You didn't show up for your shift. I covered for you but was just worried."

As he approached me for our routine kiss after work, I looked like a mess with paint all over me and my baggy denim overalls. Luckily there wasn't any on the carpeted floor.

"I'm okay. Just wasn't feeling like myself today. I got wrapped up in my art and forgot to call, that's all." I replied smiling at him.

Later that night, after calling to check in with my mother, reassuring her that I was better now, I seated myself next to Chris on the sofa as he watched the local news.

"Honey, I'm going to quit work for a while. I think I need the break." I professed.

"I figured as much, baby. You should paint again like you were doing today; you always enjoyed it." He said in return. "I will let my uncle know in the morning. Everyone will understand, but they will miss seeing you there every day."

"Thanks, Chris. I knew you'd understand." I replied as I kissed him on our way to bed.

All week, went smoothly, as I painted every day occupying my mind just as Mother told me to do. The hunger for blood eased.

That one precise evening, just as Chris was getting home, hunger hit me again at its worst, or what I thought to be the blood hunger. Falling over across my canvas in horrible pain in my stomach, I screamed out. Chris rushed to my side to help me. He took me to the hospital across the city. After two hours of waiting, we finally saw a doctor. To conclude, I was pregnant. Chris was thrilled. I, on the other hand, was in shock, and afraid.

I knew this was going to be our downfall, it had to be. Understand, I was happy and excited about having a baby, it was this 'struggle' I was worried about. Remembering all the words my mother said to me about my father after I was born, I was terrified I would do the same to my husband.

During all the months of my pregnancy, the hunger for blood ceased. Chris showered so much affection over me that it was ridiculous. I must admit, I was well pleased during this time but annoyed at the same time. So caught up in 'baby talk' I almost forgot the 'struggle'.

Chris and I were giddy as we prepared for our baby to arrive. Some days I was frustrated and moody but wasn't sure why. My emotions were like a rollercoaster during these few months. We went shopping, buying baby clothes for a little girl mostly, but we bought a few boy clothes just in case. We agreed that we wanted a baby girl, but we would still love a baby boy if that were the case.

As I got closer to my delivery date, I felt more fearful. I kept weighing it in my mind that I must tell Chris about this whole situation, but my mother disagreed, along with the worry of giving birth to my first child.

Battling it over and over in my head, it was almost driving me crazy. Chris was being so good to me during this whole pregnancy. He assumed it was just my emotions getting the better of me. I felt guilty a little as I watched him work in the guest bedroom for hours every evening preparing a nursery for our baby. He wouldn't let me even sneak a peek at it until after the baby comes home. He assured me that I would love it.

He deserved to know the truth, especially if I might murder him after our child's birth. I decided I was going to tell him, no matter what his reaction would be. He had to know about my 'struggle'. He was so good to me all the time, never complaining to me about anything, and being incredibly supportive. I owed him that much. He needed to know the truth.

The night I planned to reveal my secret, Chris had come home from the gallery with a dozen blood-red crimson roses and a bottle of ginger ale. I almost cried. He was such a romantic, and always wanted me to feel loved, he knew I was obsessed with roses. I would always paint red roses in every painting I created, and the ginger ale was in place of champagne, my favorite.

He told me that he knew I was going through so much, so he only wanted to lift my spirits. I did cry at this point.

"Aw, baby. Don't cry. "He begged. "I know, let's get you some fresh air tonight. It's a beautiful, pleasant night. Why don't we go sit in the park and look at the stars for just a bit."

"That'd be nice," I responded.

As we settled on the little white, wooden park bench, all snuggled in each other's arms, my thoughts are still on telling him the truth.

Gazing at the lovely, darkened sky with the sparkling stars shining brightly like small diamonds, I was at true peace next to him. I knew this wouldn't last after our child is born, but I was trying to enjoy this one moment, even if it was a one-time experience.

Thinking to myself, I decided I was just going to tell him, just blurt it out.

"Chris, I want to tell you something. You're probably not going to understand it fully, but I must be honest with you.

Looking at me with a bewildered face, he sat there silently.

"I have a curse on me, within my blood. I call it my 'struggle'." I openly admitted.

"A curse? What are you talking about, baby?" Chris asked in confusion as he scratched the top of his head with a small chuckle of laughter.

"Please, just be quiet and listen. I know it's going to sound bizarre, but it's the truth. I am not joking around right now." I firmly said. "As I said, it's a curse. I have a type of blood flowing in my veins that has been passed on to me since my birth. It runs within my mother's body as well. Sounds insane, but it's vampire blood."

"Vampire blood? Are you being serious right now?" He asked in a non-believing tone, giving another little snicker.

"I'm being very serious, Chris. Now, listen to me. I'm going to tell you how it all happened."

After explaining the entire tale of my mother, my father, and the night I was born, I began telling him my fears. I openly confessed it all to him. Telling him how I was afraid I would kill him after the birth of our baby and explaining more in detail about the blood hunger I was having. Though they've stopped, for now, I commenced to tell him that they could start again at any moment, especially after the baby is born, being much more severe each time they occur. I expressed my feelings to him on how I did not want the same fate for him, as happened to my father. I even explained in detail that my mother was undead.

Staring into his eyes as he sat there speechless, I spoke, "Please, say something. It's all the truth. This is real, Chris."

"I believe you, Jess, I think." He said, slothfully. "Just give me a second to take all this in."

Before he could say anything more, I screamed out, as pain so fierce coursed through my body. This pain was not from blood hunger. It was something entirely different. Falling from the little bench to the cold ground, I felt as if I couldn't breathe. I felt as if I was going to suffocate.

Chris rushed me to the hospital again. Taking me straight back, the nurses acknowledged I was in full labor. This baby was coming a month early, it was coming tonight. Screaming for Chris to call my mother, they rushed me to the labor unit.

Hours later, we have a beautiful, remarkable baby girl. Holding her in my arms, as I looked at her fragile, porcelain-like face, I couldn't imagine loving something so much. Chris and Mother were standing next to me, smiling. She was so amazing, her pale skin, her tiny fingers, and her bright blue eyes. Even her fuzzy shade of blonde hair was so adorable. She resembled her dad so much. Looking up at Chris, I told him, "She's our little ray of sunshine, our Baby Aurora Ann."

Smiling as a tear rolled down his cheek, he leaned over kissing my forehead, as we both gazed in amazement at our little girl, our small bundle of such joy.

After a week passed, we were all settled in at home, just the three of us. Mother would make an appearance every night to check in on us. Chris never spoke a word about my confession to him. Since the blood hunger urges weren't showing any signs of coming, I felt it best to stay quiet about it, and just enjoy our special time with Baby Aurora.

In my mind, I couldn't help but remember my mother's story of how she said it was only a few days after my birth that she snapped and attacked my father. It haunted me knowing that any day now I could attack Chris.

Chris finally allowed me access to see the room he had finished after our return a few short days from the hospital. Holding Baby Aurora in my arms he led me to the room. He had decorated the guest bedroom like a baby nursery with pink and yellow on the walls and stuffed teddy bears throughout the room. A gorgeous white finished baby bed was set up in the center with pink blankets and sheets. A small white wicker bassinet was placed next to a white wooden rocking chair in the corner of the nursery with a pastel pink baby blanket draped over it. Everything was perfect for our little bundle of sweetness. The room was so elegant I think I cried.

Spending unforgettable days in this nursery holding, rocking, and feeding Baby Aurora, we both cherished every second. Life was going very well, with happiness and love.

Then it finally happened. Late one night as I was standing next to Baby Aurora gazing at her in her bassinet, this hunger arose. It was by far the worst, much stronger, more extreme, almost unbearable just as Mother had said about hers, trying to overcome this blood lust feeling, I tried running as quietly, as fast as I could outside, not wanting to wake Chris. I was trying to get as far away as I could from him. But to no avail, he met me at the front door, stopping me, trying to console me, to help me. I begged and screamed, pleaded for him to get away from me, but he wouldn't listen.

The sound of the baby crying caught his attention, and he rushed to check on Baby Aurora. He never reached his destination. I attacked him from behind so fast I felt like I was a crazed animal in pursuit of my next meal. Burying my teeth so deep into the vein in his neck. As I tasted this blood for the first time, I was oblivious to anything around me. The blood was so satisfying, so hypnotizing. I lost all control of my human nature.

Hearing his heartbeat slowing, it brought me back to my reality just in time to pull myself away from him, dropping his limp body to the carpeted floor. Standing there in shock at what I had just done, I cried out in a state of agony, "No! Chris! I told you to get away from me!"

Falling to my knees, I cried out even louder, all the while, Baby Aurora was crying in the next room. What have I done? I can't let it happen this way!

That's when the thought, the idea occurred to me, I can fix this, or at least I think I can. It had to be worth the try, he's going to die either way.

Biting the vein in my wrist making the blood drip, I quickly placed my wrist on Chris's mouth. Screaming for this to work, he finally moved. He bit down so hard on my flesh that it pulled me over. Greedily, he drank blood from me. Passing out cold, he fell back to the floor, as I jerked my wrist away from his lips. Just lying there, not moving.

Had I killed him anyway? Will he come back from this? It was driving me mad waiting for any type of result, any type of sound, or any sort of movement.

Sitting next to him holding his seemingly lifeless hand in mine, crying, for what seemed like hours, yet it was only seconds, I heard the front door slam behind me. It was my mother. I will never forget the look across her troubled face as she dropped down beside me, embracing me in her arms.

"Oh, Jess, I'm so sorry." Mother only said as she continued to hold me in her arms.

Not responding, I only sat there in a daze, speechless, as I stared at Chris lying on the floor with blood all over his face, and his neck.

As mother released me, she stood pulling me up with her.

"Jess, sweetie, we have to get rid of his body." She explained.

Before I could say anything back to her, Chris slowly rose into a sitting position.

"What did you do, Jessica Lynn? He's not dead!" Mother gasped.

Rushing back down to my husband, I hugged him as tight as I could. He looked at me in amazement, shock, and confusion.

I smiled as he said, "So, you were telling me the truth about your so-called 'struggle'."

Laughing a small chuckle as I shed a tear down my cheek, I helped him up. Facing my mother, I told her what I did and how I had done it.

"Mother, I tried it. Just like in the movies, and it worked. Since it's vampire blood inside me, I figured I'd turn him instead of letting him die."

Mother just shook her head, grinning, as she said, "It worked. I can't believe it worked. That's it, you are all coming to live with me in the woods. I will not accept rejection. You're both going to need my help and my teachings on what you have become. But first, Chris needs blood. I will take him with me. Jess, you, and Baby Aurora pack some things up and meet us at the house. Hurry, before daylight comes. I know you won't hurt your baby; her blood won't tempt you, Jess, trust me I know. Now go get your baby and comfort her crying.

Leaving, Mother and Chris made their way hand in hand to find blood, or more like Mother pulling him behind her. The thoughts hit me about how they were going to obtain such blood. Mother was right, I was going to need her help with all this. The mere thought of taking a human life for their blood was going to be hard for me. I wonder how Chris is going to manage how to end a human life and drink the blood, yet I feel he will adapt better than expected. Much better than I would, I'm sure.

So, you see, this is how I became immortal. How I overcame myself, my humanity, and my 'struggle'. How I found love and happiness, and how our lives changed in one night.

As time passed on, Chris, Baby Aurora, and I converted to our new lifestyle. Chris grew wiser and adjusted quite well to being a vampire. He even expressed to me that feeding wasn't so bad after a few times of tasting the satisfying and fulfilling blood once it hits your lips. Even the guilt of taking a human's life eases after a moment.

He opened the art gallery in town extending it to be open during the night hours, with his uncle running it during the day. He explained and convinced his uncle that it was better for the business to stay open around the clock.

Mother seemed extremely happy being with us every night. We hired a 'nanny' to watch over Baby Aurora every day, as we slept. This babysitter was under the impression we worked on the graveyard shift at the gallery. I continued to work at the art gallery, but only three nights a week, while my mother helped on those nights watching Baby Aurora.

My first night feeding was hard, but with my mother helping me, I naturally adjusted to it. It comes easily enough now.

Mother took me to a deserted dirt road deep in the woods across town where only one house was visible from the road. There was a man with a hooded jacket creeping around this abandoned house. He looked to be trying to break into it, but it didn't seem feasible since no one lived in it. Mother said this would be perfect for your first victim for you to take. Agreeing with her, I prepared myself for my first take at blood other than my husband that dreadful night.

Instinct arose within me like an animal stalking its prey taking my body over, I instinctively figured out what to do. I closed in on this man so fast that he never saw me coming. Burying my fangs in his neck I drained his wretched body of every drop of blood he had. Chris was right, the blood was so satisfying and fulfilling, I felt in ecstasy for only a moment.

After that night, the feeding process got much easier. Guilt would pass after moments of being filled with the warm blood of a human. Mother and I would rotate with Chris on our feeding schedule of blood. Some nights I would stay with the baby while Mother and Chris fed. Mother wouldn't allow us to feed alone until we were stronger in controlling the blood cravings after draining our victims of their blood.

My thoughts are constantly on Baby Aurora. I know one day she will face this wretched curse, this 'struggle'. Who knows when the hunger for blood will descend on her, but I know one thing is for sure, we will all be there for her when it does. She will have her mother, her father, and her grandmother beside her for all her days on this earth. When the time is right, I will tell her the stories, the same as my mother did for me. I will tell her the whole tale, of my mother, my father, and what happened with her father and me. I will not deny her finding love. I will only plead for her to wait until she is older, mature enough, and strong enough to manage it all.

I can rest easily enough within my conscience knowing that my baby girl can now experience the delightful childhood I had here in these isolated woods. In this country home with its many features of nature and beauty. Having her own adventures and imagination. I would make sure she had as close as a normal childhood as I could.

Especially, now that we have the newfound knowledge that the one person, she falls in love with doesn't have to be murdered, but they can live together forever.

Carrying on with this undead life among mortals, I continued to enjoy my employment at the art gallery. Coming to work one evening I found a little paperback poetry book lying on my station.

So, I picked it up out of curiosity and browsed through it. It appeared to be a dark poetry book, probably left behind by someone who toured the gallery. One poem caught my eye. It read as follows...

Blood of a Vampire

Blood runs cold as ice within my veins

Flowing like a river, never to drain.

Never to love, never to feel.

Eternity for one such as I is real.

Loneliness within this vastness

Closes my eyes to my reality,

As this blood runs through with fastness

Finding the blood of a vampire isn't just a formality.

After reading this poem, it struck my heart. I honestly can relate to the words in this poem! On occasion, I feel loneliness in the mere thought of eternity, never dying. I know my little family will always be with me, but it seems overwhelming at times. When thinking and pondering on the word 'forever' it can be depressing when I realize it is my reality.

Someday in the future of this vast eternity, we can find a possible cure for this 'struggle' for us, to understand it more. Maybe, find out exactly where it came from and from whom it came. Until then, we will survive and never again have to kill the ones we love so deeply. Merely, just killing to survive as the species we are. Vampires.

The End

The Vampire's Betrayal

The Vampire's Betrayal
Part 1: Lust Games

The Vampire's Betrayal

Part 1: Lust Games

Desire... the one thing I crave more than blood. Lust and money can become an addiction. The feeling of pleasure to one's own body can make one forget all the emptiness, the loneliness, and the eternal damnation of one's soul, if my soul still exists. The ecstasy of the warm blood as it runs down my throat, as I hear the faint beating of my victim's heart. This is my story...

Being immortal has its moments of being victorious, yet it brings such guilt for a short moment. I'm Veronica. I am an immortal such as this. I'm currently residing in Manhattan, New York within the luxurious walls of The Ritz-Carlton Hotel near Times Square, practically living in room 704. The surrounding attractions lure tourists to this massive abode, such as the Empire State Building, the Museum of Modern Art, and many other nice restaurants where the wealthy can throw their money away. This location is exactly where my story begins, where I do my best seductions, and where I find my prey.

Being petite and beautiful with brown, wavy hair barely touching my shoulder and eyes of the purest green, I taunt the tourists as they pass through in this little hotel bar. Basically, it's a nightly routine. I patiently wait for someone who is alone and looks to be slightly rich. I sip my wine in a fancy glass, although it has a bittersweet taste, as I watch the people come and go. Unfortunately, I cannot read their thoughts, that's the one undead gift I do not possess. Dwelling at the mahogany bar with the dim lights above, I cautiously scan the small crowd of drunken individuals.

One such person catches my eye. He's a distinguished gentleman that looks to be in his late forties. His frame appears to be slightly muscular underneath his dark blue, tailored suit with hair as black as night. He seems average yet expensive as he drinks his bourbon on ice. He must be a man of some importance. Gently picking my wine glass up, I flirtatiously stroll over to his table. Our eyes meet as I place myself across from him...

"So, are you visiting or are you here on business?" I seductively ask as I continue to look into his eyes sipping my red wine.

Coughing a nervous cough, he answered in an Italian accent, "Just business, pretty lady. May I ask who you are?"

"I'm Veronica, sir," I replied. "I can make your wildest dreams a reality, at least for one evening."

Smiling, the man nodded his head and asked, "Exactly, how are you supposed to do that? Besides, you look to be about twenty years of age."

"Trust me, sir, I'm well beyond twenty years old." I stated as I grinned an evil grin taking another sip of my bitter wine.

It wasn't much longer into this petty conversation, I had him in my grasp.

Caressing in a heated, lustful passion, we made our way up to the seventh floor to my suite. Passing through the hotel door to my spacious room, clothes began coming off. This man's intense body was stunning! His muscle tone was almost perfect. As he stared lustfully into my green eyes, I slowly pushed him onto the queen-sized bed with satin sheets. Climbing on top of his well-toned form, I straddled his hard, masculine manliness. He groaned in pleasure as I forcefully squeezed my thighs into him. I began to caress his bare chest with my fingertips as I leaned into his strong embrace. His massive arms held my naked, cold body against his warm, male physique. Slowly and playfully, I commenced kissing his neck in the area I intended on piercing with my sharp teeth. Thrusting harder as I held him in my grasp.

One fatal bite and he would be no more, but I only had a small taste to sustain my evil convictions. He yelled in a loud fright as he reached his final climax. I could feel the sweat of his body as he shoved me from his embrace. He jumped to his feet grabbing his clothes from the floor as he stumbled trying to escape to the door. He held his hand over his bloody neck as he screamed for help.

Smiling wickedly, I rubbed my tongue over my lips as I enjoyed the sensation of his blood. My naked frame felt warm and tremendously well pleased. I sprang to my feet before he could actually reach the doorway catching this man before he even knew I had him. I gripped his shoulder as I placed my hand over his eyes making him wilt to the floor in a comatose state. I hadn't any choice but to erase his memory, clear his mind of this situation. He was being entirely too loud with his panicking. Dragging his limp body back to the bed I gently placed his clothing back onto his figure. I quickly draped a robe over my bare skin and grabbed a warm towel from the bathroom. Cleaning his neck from any signs of blood, I decided to get my funds from his wallet placing it back into his pants pocket. I eased him in a sitting position snapping my fingers in front of his face. He awakened instantly. In a state of confusion he asked, "Who the hell are you? Why am I in this room?"

I kindly explained to him as I caressed his cheek with my fingers, "We had met in the little bar downstairs. We had drinks and you had one too many, so, I brought you to my room to help you sober up. We were supposed to have sex, but you passed out during our actual intercourse."

Shaking his head, confused, he never responded. He stood in bewilderment and made his exit.

So, you see, this is how I manage to stay fed and survive. Mostly, nightly, but some evenings, I seduce them right in the bar or in a corner, taking just enough blood to sustain myself. I crave the blood, yet I crave the pleasure more on some nights. Of course, there is times I have to wipe their entire memory of me leaving them in a zombie state. Some live, some die. It's very rare I actually murder anyone, but when the need arises, I haven't a choice. Some of my desirable victims can become violent or afraid and I cannot deal with such rudeness. You see, I never take their life in my hotel room, I only drain them enough to hypnotize their brain to do something fatal after they leave my presence.

The sexual pleasure, the ecstasy of the blood, and the joy of the game makes me feel powerful, invincible. I love to feel desired and wanted by my victims. I enjoy watching them struggle to get away from me once they see my true nature, yet I never reveal my fangs until

I get my full orgasm from them. Do I only seduce the rich men? Of course not, I enjoy the financially stable ladies that seem lonely and power hungry in their stressful careers. The ones who work all the time never having any time for enjoyment. Those are the ones who I have to put out a strong effort to lure back to my dwelling. The challenge is mystifying to me.

One such instance was on a stormy night. The rain was brutally falling outside. The little bar was in a miserable state, yet there was a handful of people mingling about. As I rested my face in my hands, I overheard a woman ask the bartender for a weird drink. This female ordered a cranberry and vodka with a splash of bourbon on ice. This struck my curiosity. I wasn't in a hunger for blood since I had fed only hours ago on a fine gentleman that dwelt in the corner booth of the bar. This lady's blood stirred my senses. I knew right away from her mere demeanor that she was going to be tough. I had to have her; I had to taste her.

After this lady placed herself in a seat at the bar, just a few chairs from me, I watched her sip her drink as she put some papers on the counter in front of her. It appeared she was in some type of marketing or sales. She was fully focused on her work material, so, I decided to ease closer to her. Relocating in the leather chair right next to her, I ordered a red wine from the bartender, which was my usual order. Nonchalantly taking a sip of my wine, I quietly cleared my throat and said, "So, are you here on a business trip or just passing through?"

The woman looked at me as she graciously nodded her head and went back to sipping her drink while reading her paperwork. I knew right then that this was going to be slightly a tough one. This casual lady wasn't even remotely interested in my presence. Catching the bartender's attention, I ordered another of her strange drinks since I noticed she was almost finished with the one she had. This little gesture triggered her attention as she respectfully declined, saying, "Thank you, miss, but I think I'm finished drinking for the evening."

"Are you quite sure, my lady?" I returned with a seductive question as I shyly winked my eye at her. "I mean, it is a rainy, dreadful night and it's a perfect time to let loose from working. You seem like the type of person who overworks herself on a daily basis. Besides, everyone needs a 'good time' at least once in their life."

After pulling her long, blonde hair into a ponytail, the lady began gathering her papers and putting them into a briefcase. Stopping suddenly, she took a deep breath and exhaled. This determined woman looked straight at me as she rolled her eyes and accepting the drink. I smiled wickedly.

After several hours of drinking and conversating childishly about this lady's stressful career, I finally convinced this overworked woman to accompany me to my room. She was extremely intoxicated now, so, my seduction would be smooth like a breeze. Walking arm in arm, I had to carefully balance this female as we approached the elevators.

Inside the elevator I propped her against the mahogany wall as the steel doors closed. Blowing my breath toward the ceiling of this elevator near the corner, I fogged over the security camera. Pushing the button on the elevator panel, the mechanism halted between floors. Returning my focus to this drunken lady, I quickly leaned in for a kiss. She easily kissed me back as she pulled me closer to her body. She moaned as I slid my cold hand into her suit pants straight to her warm pussy.

Please understand, she was very drunk off too many cranberries and vodkas at this point, so, I do not think she knew who or what was happening to her, or where she even was. She was breathing heavily now as I thrust my fingers inside her. I had to control myself or I would devour this mortal much too quickly. Her blood smelled so inviting to my undead senses. I could vaguely feel her intense heat between her legs as I continued to breach her moist vagina. She stiffened in a heated passion as she moaned louder. We were intertwined as in a couple's embrace as she squeezed my shoulders pulling me closer against her breasts. My lips sucked and teased her neck as I held her in place against the wall. My fangs pierced her throat as she reached her overwhelming orgasm. Her blood was so bitter from so much alcohol, but I didn't care.

After draining her of her blood almost to the point of death, I realized I had simply gained my pleasure from this being without having her touch my body in anyway. She slowly faded as her eyes closed tightly. Gently, I eased her to floor of the elevator as I cleaned the blood from her neck with my tongue. Removing my hand from her wet, forbidden area, I carefully situated this woman's attire in a proper fashion. With her limp body propped upon the wall, I felt her pulse in her wrist. There was still a heartbeat, but faintly. Deciding it best to leave her where she was, I placed my hand over her shut eyes and cleared all her memory of meeting me. Pushing the button on the elevator switchboard, I hit the number seven. I figured someone would mingle into this elevator eventually to find this poor mortal. If she survives, it would strictly be up to her.

I left this beautiful lady in the floor of the elevator as I made my way to my secluded room feeling full and completely satisfied. So, you see, this is how my lonely, undead life goes damn near on a nightly basis. I must admit, I enjoy the painful, yet amazing seduction, the misleading, the playfulness of the game, and the mystery of luring these mortals into my evil grasp. It's almost too easy sometimes. I've remained in this hotel for four years and never has anyone been suspicious of my seductions. I've relocated many times over the centuries, yet this place is definitely my favorite dwelling.

Everything seemed to be going great in the world of seducing these unaware mortals until one late evening when I saw him, Matthew. When I saw his narrow face glistening in the pale light of the barroom, a feeling shot through my entire undead body. This warm feeling was unlike anything I'd ever felt, but before I tell this part of my tale, I have one more 'lust' game I'd like to share...

On some nights, I find it is exciting, thrilling, to lure two, maybe three, mortals at a time back to my apartment. One such instance comes to mind that went considerably wrong. I was lingering, as usual, in the little hotel bar one late evening drinking my red wine as best I could at the end of the bar, when I noticed a small group of local college students mingle their way into the establishment. They were already strongly intoxicated and boldly asking the bartender for some whiskey shots. After consuming their shots, I watched them seat themselves at a corner table. Seemingly, several moments slipped by as a few of the students made their leave with only the two guys and one girl still sitting at the wooden table. They were flirting with each other in a sexy way as the girl with the long braids playfully kissed the guy with the wavy black hair.

Thinking to myself, "Should I join them and get in on the fun?"

Deciding I would try, I gracefully approached these loud adolescents, placing my glass of wine onto their table as I eased into the seat next to the guy with blonde curly hair. Looking concerned, the girl with the awful braids asked, "Who the hell are you? Why are you seating yourself at our table? This is a private function."

I could see the blonde male was very interested in my presence, but the selfish girl was skittish of me.

"Well, my lady, I'd like to join you in your fun, if I may. Should I buy a round of drinks?" I responded seductively.

"We can afford our own drinks, miss, but thanks anyway." The dark-haired male answered as he continued kissing the girl's neck.

I could tell this girl was a little bothered by my presence since it seemed as if she wanted these two guys for herself tonight. So, I hastily said, "No worries. I only wanted to partake in this playful seduction. I have a nice room on the seventh floor if you guys would like to move the party upstairs."

The strange girl quickly responded, "No thanks", telling me they were 'just leaving' as she grabbed the male's hand with the dark hair and motioning for the smiling, blonde male to follow her.

As they made their exit, I cautiously followed behind them. The challenge intrigued me, I suppose. Besides, I was not very fond of this smartass girl.

I noticed they were heading straight to Central Park as they stumbled over each other trying to keep their drunken balance. Watching as the girl leaned against an oak tree with the black-haired male teasingly seducing her, I realized that the other male was just sitting on the grass at their feet gazing at them with lustful eyes. I figured this was my chance! Quietly, I eased up to the blonde male, placing my arms around his waist as I lifted him from the ground. He freely gave in to my embrace as he kissed my cold, moist lips.

"I knew you wanted me." This blonde-haired mortal whispered as he continued to kiss my neck.

The two lovers against the tree gave no interest, only continued with their passionate lovemaking. As I began kissing this guy, I slowly caressed his dick in his thick jeans while he moaned in pure pleasure, all the while his dick getting extremely hard. Sucking on my neck, this male began touching and rubbing me as he tried to reach my forbidden vagina. He was trying to please me by caressing my heated area. I must admit, he was not very good at it. Finally, I had enough for tonight!

This just wasn't satisfying my own dark desires; besides, we were out in public, and it was much too acceptable to be noticed by someone. Deciding it best to end this boring seduction, I brutally yet quietly, drained this blonde-haired male of his blood dropping him to the dampened grass. Quickly, I gripped the dark-haired guy as I held tightly to the girl's throat against the tree. Sucking the blood from this male until he fell limp to the dirty ground. Turning my focus to the braided haired girl that I held in my grasp, I placed my hand over her eyes as she screamed in fear. I figured I would erase her memory while I sank my fangs into her warm flesh. When I felt this girl weaken in my arms, I dropped her to the grass next to her lover.

Leaving the three college students where they lay, I made my way back to the hotel. I'm not sure why I had to have those mortals, but at first, I was interested. Somewhere along the way, I lost that interest and decided to just have their blood instead of their pleasures. It seems the older mortals with better sexual experiences fulfill my lustful desire much better. The younger ones seem to be too bold and more aggressive in their seductions, much too demanding. Although, their blood was satisfying yet it was bitter from all the alcohol consumption they had partaken in.

I believe it was the challenge of these younger mortals that intrigued me. I just can't stand rejection! The disrespect of that braided-haired girl made me slightly furious. I haven't a clue rather those mortals lived or died. Part of me did not care. This experience was the only time I had trouble getting an orgy party together. Most of the time, it was quite a breeze to lure a group of older mortals back to my room to enjoy a lustful, romantic feast.

Now, I will tell my small tale of Matthew. The one male that gave me a great challenge to seduce him. Like I said earlier, I first saw him at the hotel bar that late evening and had a strange, warm sensation go throughout my undead body.

Part 2: The Courtship

Part 2: The Courtship

I could see this mortal male was different from all the others I had seduced. I could sense his blood was strange, yet I knew he was a human. It intrigued me. I wanted to taste his blood and feel it spread throughout my undead body. I started feeling a strong yearning for this mysterious guy to touch my forbidden area with his masculine hands, to feel his lips kiss my breasts as he caressed my entire body. This sensation was about to madden me when I heard him order a beer from the bartender. Watching him for a short moment, I tried to study his muscular figure through his attire.

It appeared to my imaginations that his body frame was slightly toned and well-fit. Everything in me wanted to stroll my fingers and palms across his entire body. I wanted to slowly touch him, I wanted to taste him and his blood, and I wanted to place my lips onto his masculine domain. I assumed his dick was of a nice quality and size and would give the exact amount of lustful pleasure that my undead body needed. I wanted to feel his warmth upon my cold, chilled skin and feel his manhood enter my moist, throbbing vagina as he kissed my freezing lips with his heated passion.

Blinking my eyes a few times as if to snap out of this overheated seduction in my mind bringing me back to reality, I decided to casually make my way to the mahogany bar where this gorgeous male was seated. He was sipping on his cold beer as he stared off into space in deep thought. It was driving me crazy to know what he was thinking!

Ordering another glass of red wine, I cautiously asked this guy, "Why such deep thoughts?"

Turning his head to look at me, he only nodded with a crooked grin as he returned to his private gaze, tasting his alcoholic beverage. Rolling my eyes, it frustrated me! I wanted him to speak to me, at least, acknowledge my presence with a form of gratitude, but he was severely wrapped up in his own depressing mind!

After dwelling next to him in this leather bar chair for what felt like hours, I finally broke the silence, and spoke to him again.

"I'm Veronica." I said boldly. "Who might you be? Are you from around here or just travelling through?"

Placing his beer bottle onto the bar, he answered in a determined tone as he looked right at me, "I'm Matthew, and my business is my own."

"Well, excuse me! I meant no rudeness to you, sir. I just wanted to make 'small' talk since you seem to be the only person in this secluded bar that offered an interesting type of conversation tonight."

"Understandable, Miss Veronica." He said sarcastically. "But I'd rather be alone, if you don't mind."

Catching the rude hint, I only smiled as I graciously took my glass of wine and made my way back to my usual little table in the darkened corner of the room. This was going to be tough, but I would not give up until I had this 'Matthew' before this night was over. I just needed to watch him a little longer, maybe try to figure out what intrigues this strange man. It maddened me, yet engrossed my senses as to why this guy was not remotely interested in me. I was beautiful, sexy, and confident. So, why was this guy not falling into my seduction?

Confused, I stared straight at him. I knew he could feel my stare. Finally, he glances over at me, showing no expression as he returned to his private gaze while continuing to finish his second beer. Frustrated within myself at this point, I walked hastily, straight up to him placing my wine glass hard onto the wooden bar right next to him.

"I can see you are some kind of a 'loner', but there is no need to be so cruelly rude and ignore me."

Laughing a small chuckle, he replied, "Well, Miss Veronica, if you must know so badly, I'm on a dreadful business trip that I do not want to be on. My boss is a jerk, and it sucks! I had no choice but to come to New York only to rip off a small company and overtake their assets. So, forgive me if I'm not in the mood to be seduced by a lovely lady on this night."

There it was. My chance to find out more about this strange man. Obviously, he was aggravated with his type of lively hood. Motioning for the bartender to bring another round of drinks, I seated myself next to him as I slid his beer in front of him. Accepting the beer, Matthew said, "Thanks for the beer."

"You're welcome." I smugly replied as I smiled. "Seems you could use one more."

"No shit." He said in return as he grinned back to me.

After several moments of awkward silence, I finally asked, "So, would you like to talk about it? I mean, I'm a complete stranger to you. I know nothing of who you are, so, I'd be a perfect candidate to hear your story."

"No, thanks. I'd rather drink my beer and try to forget my frustrations for now."

"I understand, I suppose."

Taking my hand, I gently started to play seductively with his hair on the back of his neck as I moved my body close to his.

"I could ease your mind if you allow me to. Make you forget about your frustrations for the rest of the evening." I whispered in his ear in a sexual, quiet tone as I leaned in to kiss his fragile lips, trying to seduce this man as best I could.

Slamming his beer bottle onto the bar, he stood quickly, pushing me away from him as he stated, "No thanks, but I appreciate the offer."

Unfortunately, I watched him walk away feeling maddened, rejected. This was honestly the first victim I ever lost. It frustrated me but I did not want to kill him just yet. He was too mysterious to rid him of his life at this point. Oh, how I hated rejection! Deciding I would secretly follow him, I noticed he went to the elevator getting off at the 5th floor of this hotel. So, that's when I returned to the bar to await a mortal of less interest. I would angrily devour a few mortals this night out of mere frustration. At least, I now know he's within this building, but for how long would be the important question.

I found myself dwelling, lingering, in the little bar over several nights without feasting or feeling any type of pleasures, all in hopes of this 'Matthew' coming back. I even walked to the 5th floor of the hotel on a few occasions trying to locate his room. No such luck! I felt like I was becoming obsessed, like a type of crazed stalker.

Finally, one late night, I was sitting in my normal spot in the corner of the bar still thinking about Matthew, when it happened. He walked into the bar and seated himself in the leather chair ordering a whiskey shot and a beer.

Part 3: Love or Lust?

Part 3: Love or Lust?

That particular late night changed my immortal life, my viscous routine, for an eternity. I wasn't quite sure if it was actual love or just mere lust, but I knew this Matthew was not all that interested in me. It bothered me greatly. I hated to be rejected. I had to have him physically, mentally, and lustfully. Of course, it was a challenge but eventually I succeeded. I believe this actual challenge is what lured me to him. Was it just pure lust or was it actually love? Guess it will forever be a mystery. This is the tale of how I overtook my Matthew...

As I pondered on the idea of ripping Matthew's throat out as I watched him sip his beer at the bar across the room from me, I felt angered. How could he just reject my presence, my proposal, and my beauty? It was becoming personal now; I would have him. I didn't care if it meant killing him. He would be mine. I was determined at this point.

Deciding to make my presence known again to him this night, I slowly eased over seating myself at the bar just a few chairs from him. I ordered something different than my usual drink, a bourbon on ice. I began gazing in his general direction as to be obvious. The bourbon was extremely sour to my taste, but it seemed to keep me calm.

As he continued to sip on his cold beer, I slowly eased my agitation. As I was about to speak in his direction, Matthew spoke first. He turned his head looking straight at me....

"Look, Miss Veronica, I want to be left alone." He stated boldly. "But, if you are so intent on seducing me, let's get it over with. Where is your room? Shall we go?"

He stood grinning a crooked smile toward me as he held out his hand in a gesture for me to get up. Laughing to myself, thinking this seems too easy, I graciously took his hand leading him toward the elevators. I felt I had won this challenge, yet I knew he didn't exactly want me. I understood it was only 'lust' for him, but I did not care. I would claim this victory!

Entering my room, I quickly embraced Matthew before he could change his mind, kissing him very passionately that it seemed to have shocked him. He began kissing me back, but with much more force. Our clothes began falling off as we fell onto the queen-size bed. Pressing his nicely toned body against mine, I stopped him, suggesting we first take a romantic bath in the little porcelain tub in the bathroom.

Rolling his eyes at me, he patiently waited for the warm water to fill the tub. His erection was so intense as he stood next to me against the counter. I slowly stepped into the bathtub turning the water off, seating myself in the refreshing water. I began caressing my breasts while he watched. Taunting him to join me in the water, he was reaching the point of explosion. Viciously, Matthew pulled me from the water carrying me back to the bed. He whispered in my ear, "Pleasuring oneself can be extremely seductive and fascinating!"

I could tell he was very much tempted and turned on. I had completed my job in luring him in. Tossing me onto the messed-up bed, he hastily placed himself on top of my wet, cold, naked body. His skin was extremely moist, hot, and sweaty. This aroused my senses. Reaching for the pillowcase next to my head, I ripped it off the pillow as I placed it around Matthew's eyes holding it tightly. I wanted to be more seductive, more playful, but he torturously ripped it from my grasp, saying, "No. I want to see all of you."

Looking at me as if he could see straight to my undying soul, he started to tease my nipples with his fingers. He whispered to me, "Your breasts are so porcelain-like and your nipples are simply beautiful."

Before I could reply, he roughly began sucking my nipples and teasing them with his heated tongue. They were so hard and perky; it would've been too much pain for a mortal woman. Lust was coursing through my undead body; unlike any I've ever experienced. This mortal male knew how to arouse and pleasure a woman! Suddenly, I felt like my body would explode!

He placed his massive, hardened dick into my heated, wet vagina. I could feel his entire body tense up as he unloaded his manhood inside me. During this ecstasy, I totally forgot I was immortal and how much I wanted to taste his blood. Lying next to one another and feeling completely satisfied, I started to smell the scent of his blood, but my body was still in a type of limbo, ecstasy.

Matthew drifted into a deep sleep as I lay next to him just staring at his fragile face. He was such a beautiful man. It's a shame that I may have to feast on him very soon. The blood running through his vein was becoming so unbearable to my immortal senses. Right at the point where I was going to bite his neck, he woke up.

Stopping myself from piercing his vein, I only kissed him on his neck. He lifted my head placing his lips to mine. After a brief moment of sexual intimacy, Matthew stood and began placing his clothes back on, saying, "Let's get a drink at the bar now. I need a strong one."

Not responding to him, I followed his lead. Getting dressed; I accompanied him to the little bar downstairs. Ordering two bourbons on ice, we sat at the mahogany bar, neither of us speaking a word. Just gazing at this masculine man, I smiled. I was dwelling on how he had pleasured me only moments ago. No mortal has ever pleased me in this way! I pondered on why I haven't taken all his blood yet. Maybe, I felt funny, like a mortal lady that was falling in some type of love. Matthew stared straight in front of himself as I knew he felt my intense stare. It was obvious that he was pondering about our sexual encounter too. Before I could break the silence between us to ask about his thoughts, this petite woman from across the room yells "Matthew" as she walks right up to him, saying, "There you are. I've been looking for you for hours. Where have you been?"

Without answering her, Matthew takes this woman by the arm and rushes her to the elevators leaving me alone. I became furious! That rude bastard just left me here! No explanation as to why or who this bitch was! As a monster, I was severely angered! I knew I wasn't justified to be this angry within myself, but it still infuriated me! Even though, I'm a brutal fiend, I still felt as if I had been played a 'fool' by Matthew.

Finishing my strong iced beverage with its bitter taste irritating my tongue, I slammed the glass onto the bar countertop. Leaving the little bar area, I made my way to the elevators up to the 5th floor. I knocked on every hotel door on that floor until I found Matthew's room. Maybe I was being like a mortal, jealous girl, but I was angry.

When that same petite woman opened the door, I went into a heated rage. I grabbed her by her throat as I pushed my way into the hotel room. She never had a chance to scream as my fangs pierced her vein in her neck. This poor lady never knew what had her. I drained her to her death without a drop of blood left inside her lifeless body. At this point, Matthew ran from the steaming bathroom wrapped in a towel with his body dripping wet.

"What the hell have you done?" was all he could scream as he shoved me away from this pitiful woman. Trying his best to revive her, Matthew pleaded for me to call for help as he continued to curse me excessively.

Smiling devilishly, I never said a word in response to his pleadings. I only tasted the warm blood from the victim on my lips as I watched Matthew try his best to save his dead friend. Finally, he gave up on saving her. He jumped to his feet in anger and came toward me as if to harm me for taking this woman's life.

"You murdered my wife, Veronica! What the hell were you thinking?" Matthew shouted at me as he gripped my throat, squeezing hard with both his hands trying to stop my airflow.

He was brutally strong for a mortal male, if only he knew this was pointless, I could not die! Realizing that I was not human, he stumbles back in shock or fear when he noticed my sharp fangs that still had his wife's blood dripping from them. Terrified, he turns to run for the door that was still opened, but it was useless. I swiftly attacked him from behind sinking my teeth deep into his neck.

He was completely lifeless now, gone.

Gathering Matthew and his poor wife from the carpeted floor, I gently placed their dead bodies onto the king-size bed. Making my leave, I closed the door and never returned. I left them in their room on the 5th floor to be found by someone else.

Part 4: Only Eternity

P art 4: Only Eternity

The next evening, I packed my few belongings, checked out of the hotel, and left this beautiful residence in Manhattan. My time here was interesting and fun, but I hadn't a choice but to leave. Of course, I found myself feeling 'guilt' for Matthew and his poor spouse, but I am immortal, a monster, so the feeling doesn't linger for too long.

In my unjustified defense, I find that the humanistic reality was simply this... 'The Vampire's Betrayal was more than Matthew could bare... Goodbye Matthew... It's over. It's done. It is finished, yet I feel I betrayed myself.'

Was it mere 'lust', the challenge of rejection, or could it have been 'love' that I felt for Matthew that night? I suppose it will forever be a mystery now.

I never said that my little tale was a romance. I wished it could've been, but sometimes 'love' or 'lust' can be deadly.

I now reside in London; my location and residence will remain unknown now. My memories of Manhattan and of Matthew only surface on rare occasions, yet I will always remember our intercourse of pure ecstasy. I try to forget the aftermath, but it creeps in at times.

I still feed on mortal victims who seem wealthy. I will play with such mortals in a reasonable routine on a nightly basis just as before, yet I made myself a promise to never again pursue an unwilling individual. It just isn't worth the 'guiltiness' I felt that night in New York. Rage and jealously is something I will not allow myself to ever feel again, definitely not 'love' or any type of sensual feelings for my victims from now on. I seduce, I feed, and I leave. I get my needed fill of blood and pleasure and move along.

Time fades away and it can't be stopped. One cannot change it.

I do believe now that I could've loved Matthew if it had lasted longer, and I did not act out in anger. Maybe that's why I couldn't drink his blood at first. He made me feel human again. The realization that he loved his wife was more than I could handle that night. Maybe it was just jealously on my part. Maybe it angered me to know he loved that petite woman, and I could never feel that kind of love.

Now I only have eternity to exist, as I set in this little sport pub on the outskirts of the city of London. I continue to watch these wretched mortals drink their drinks and try to hide their mixed-up emotions. I shall continue to prey on their blood and gain my personal pleasures. I shall never again let myself betray myself! I'm only existing in my eternity as an immortal beauty!

The Vampire's Betrayal

Blood & Betrayal
Anna Elizabeth
Tasha Joy

Blood & Betrayal